Let's Investigate Magical, Mysterious Meteorites

Madelyn Wood Carlisle

Illustrated by Yvette Santiago Banek

BARRON'S

All inquiries should be addressed to:
Barron's Educational Series, Inc.
250 Wireless Boulevard
Hauppauge, NY 11788

International Standard Book No. 0-8120-4733-8

Library of Congress Catalog Card No. 92-12776

Library of Congress Cataloging-in Publication Data

Carlisle, Madelyn Wood.
    Let's investigate magical, mysterious meteorites / Madelyn Wood Carlisle;
    illustration by Yvette Santiago Banek.
      p.   cm.
    Summary: Discusses the nature and origin of meteorites and relates stories
    of famous meteorites, meteorite craters, and meteor showers.
    ISBN 0-8120-4733-8
    1. Meteorites— Juvenile literature.   [1. Meteorites.]   I. Banek, Yvette Santiago,
    ill.   II. Title
    QB755.2.C37   1992
    523.5'1—dc20
                                                            92-12776
                                                               CIP
                                                                AC

PRINTED IN MEXICO
2345 8800 987654321

Contents

Visitors From Space

"Look! A shooting star!"

Have you ever cried out those words? And then made a silent wish?

There is something so mysterious and magical about a light streaking across the dark night sky that we like to think it can make a wish come true.

Of course we know a shooting star isn't really a star. It's a meteor, a rock from outer space that has entered the atmosphere of Earth.

Before a meteor comes into Earth's atmosphere it is traveling at a speed of over 100,000 miles (160,000 kilometers) an hour. The friction created when it moves through the air slows it down. Friction also makes the outer surface of the meteor so hot that it burns and melts, leaving the trail of glowing droplets that cause us to look up in wonder.

Meteors most often burn up completely or explode before they reach the surface of our planet. But some land on Earth. Once a meteor, or a part of one, has made a landing, it is called a meteorite.

So before a meteorite is a meteorite it's a meteor, and before that, when it's way out there in space, it's called a meteoroid.

Look! A shooting star!

There are many museums where you can see meteorites on display.

4

It's exciting to hold a meteorite in your hands.

This meteorite, found in New Mexico, was once molten lava somewhere out in space.

SOME MUSEUMS WHERE YOU CAN SEE METEORITES

American Museum of Natural History. New York, New York

Arizona State Museum. Tempe, Arizona

University of Arkansas Planetarium. Little Rock, Arkansas

Chesapeake Planetarium. Chesapeake, Virginia

John Deere Planetarium. Rock Island, Illinois

Denver Museum of Natural History. Denver, Colorado

Field Museum. Chicago, Illinois

Fleischmann Planetarium. Reno, Nevada

Geological Survey of Canada Museum. Ottawa, Ontario

Griffith Observatory. Los Angeles, California

Hansen Planetarium. Salt Lake City, Utah

Houston Museum of Natural Science. Houston, Texas

Institute of Meteoritics . University of New Mexico. Albuquerque, New Mexico

Mineralogical Museum of Harvard University. Cambridge, Massachusetts

National Museum of Natural History. Washington, D.C.

Pacific Science Center. Seattle, Washington

Peabody Museum of Natural History. New Haven, Connecticut

Royal Ontario Museum. Toronto, Ontario

M.Y. Williams Geological Museum. Vancouver, British Columbia

There are other museums with meteorite collections. Call your library or a museum in your city to ask for the location of the nearest display.

5

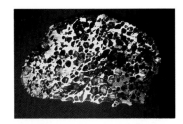

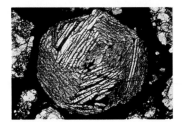

Sections of meteorites as seen through an electron microscope. Scientists know that the top meteorite came from the core of a small planet. The round spot in the second meteorite was a drop of molten lava when our solar system was forming. The bottom two are the same meteorite, photographed under different kinds of light.

There are three different kinds of meteorites. One group is metal, mostly iron and nickel. These are called iron meteorites, or just irons. Another kind is made up of stone or rock. These meteorites have no metal in them and are called stony meteorites, or just stones. In the third group are what we call the stony-irons. They contain a mixture of stone and metals.

Have you ever seen a meteorite up close? Many museums have them. If you ever have a chance to look at a meteorite, or if you can actually hold one, stop to think about how truly amazing meteorites are. They are among the only objects from outer space that we have ever seen and touched! True, astronauts brought back rocks from the moon. But the moon is practically in Earth's backyard. Meteorites come from many millions of miles away from our planet.

Scientists all over the world are studying meteorites. They cut them up, look at sections of them under microscopes and make tests to find out what chemicals, minerals, and metals they contain. They hope that these visitors from space will tell us some of the secrets of how our universe began.

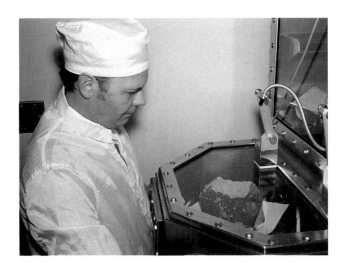

To study meteorites, scientists cut them up into slices as thin as sheets of aluminum foil.

An astronaut collecting rock samples on the moon. The moon has been hit by many meteorites.

A piece of nickel-iron meteorite found in Arizona.

Where Do Meteorites Come From?

In our solar system, Mercury is the planet closest to the sun. Then comes Venus, then Earth, then Mars. Jupiter is next, but it's a long way out. All that space between Mars and Jupiter is not just empty space. It is filled with a vast belt of particles. Some are tiny specks of dust. Others are huge rocky masses many miles across. We call them asteroids. We believe that many meteorites come from this asteroid belt.

Asteroids orbit the sun. Their orbits are not all the same, so their paths often cross. Sometimes they crash into each other.

When this happens, broken-off pieces of an asteroid can be sent whirling off into an entirely different orbit. The new piece may be just a tiny pebble or it may be as large as one of Earth's biggest mountains. Whatever its size, we call it a meteoroid.

Its new orbit may take it closer and closer to Earth. If it gets close enough it will be pulled into our atmosphere by Earth's gravity.

Someday, astronauts from Earth may bring back minerals from the asteroid belt.

When two asteroids collide and break apart, pieces of them sometimes land on Earth.

ASTEROID ANSWERS

When was the first asteroid discovered?

An Italian astronomer named Giuseppi Piazzi made the first asteroid discovery in 1801. While studying the sky on clear winter nights, Piazzi saw a faint "star" that changed its position from one night to the next. He realized that what he was seeing was a tiny planet orbiting the sun somewhere out between Mars and Jupiter. Other scientists studied Piazzi's find and soon located more miniature planets in similar orbits. They were given the name *asteroids*.

How big is the biggest asteroid?

The biggest asteroid is Ceres, the very one discovered by Piazzi. It is a spherical body about 600 miles (almost 1,000 kilometers) in diameter.

How many asteroids are there?

While over 30,000 asteroids have been located and photographed through telescopes, nobody knows how many more might be identified. Scientists guess that there may be as many as 400,000 more, most of them far too small to be seen.

Will people ever travel to the asteroid belt?

It's possible that space miners of the future will journey to the asteroid belt to mine minerals that have become scarce on Earth. Many asteroids are known to contain large quantities of metals of various kinds.

Meteorites striking the moon have sent pieces of moon rock hurtling toward Earth.

Meteorites also strike the moon and the other planets. When people first looked through telescopes, they thought that the moon's many craters had been made by volcanoes. Now we know that they were caused by meteoroids and comets.

The moon has many more craters than Earth. That is because the moon has no atmosphere to burn or break up or slow down the meteoroids that approach it.

Sometimes meteoroids hitting the moon break off pieces of moon rock. Some of these pieces of moon have landed on Earth. The largest moon meteorite found so far weighs just under 1½ pounds (680 grams). Scientists in the Antarctic picked it up off the ice. Imagine their excitement when they discovered that it exactly matched the rocks brought back from the moon by the Apollo astronauts.

Another meteorite found in the Antarctic excited them even more. They believe that it is a piece of Mars!

The moon, as seen from an Apollo spacecraft.

Meteorites that have fallen in the Antarctic are easy to see against the white snow. Scientists were excited to discover that one Antarctic meteorite is a piece of Mars. They estimate that the meteorite (both sides of which are shown above) is about 1,300 million years old.

Mars, photographed from a Viking orbiter.

Sizes and Shapes

You probably can't walk anywhere without stepping on stardust.

Meteorites fall on Earth every single day, but most are just tiny specks. You probably can't go anywhere without walking on stardust!

But of course large meteorites fall too. Many are big enough to make huge holes, or craters, in the ground. That may sound scary, but you will be happy to know that no big meteorite has ever fallen on a city, town, or building.

In between the dust-sized particles and the giants there are meteorites of many sizes. They can be round, oval, or shaped like bricks, boomerangs, hammers, or loaves of bread.

Some of the huge meteorites we find seem so special that we give them names. The biggest known meteorite in the world is called Hoba West. It landed in Africa thousands of years ago. Scientists think it weighs about 120,000 pounds (54,000 kilograms). Many large meteorites are moved from where they were found and taken to museums so that more people can see them. But Hoba West still rests in its desert landing place.

Found in Norton County, Kansas, this meteorite weighs about a ton. The apple enables you to estimate its size.

Indians in Oregon called the Willamette meteorite "Visitor from the Moon" and believed it had magical powers.

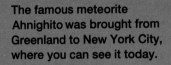

The famous meteorite Ahnighito was brought from Greenland to New York City, where you can see it today.

The biggest meteorite ever found in the United States weighs 28,000 pounds (12,700 kilograms). It is called Willamette because it landed in the Willamette Valley in Oregon. The Clackamas Indians called it "Tomanowos," or "Visitor From the Moon," and believed it had magical powers. Before going into battle, the warriors dipped their arrows and washed their faces in the rainwater that collected in hollows in the huge stone from the sky.

If you live in New York City, or ever go there, you can see Willamette in the American Museum of Natural History. There you can also see—and even touch—68,000-pound (30,800 kilogram) Ahnighito. Later in this book you will read the story of how this giant meteorite was moved from Greenland to New York.

Has Anyone Ever Been Hit by a Meteorite?

An Indiana boy named Brodie Spaulding was standing in his front yard on an August day in 1991 when he heard a whistling noise and saw a fist-sized rock hit the ground a few feet away from him. Chemists who analyzed the rock said it was a meteorite, all right, and that Brodie was lucky it hadn't hit him instead of the ground.

Brodie is one of the few people who has actually seen a meteorite fall to Earth. Scientists joke that if you were to stand out in a field with a basket in your hands, hoping that a meteorite would fall into it, you would probably have to wait one and a half billion years before you caught one! As far as we know, no one has ever been killed or even seriously injured by a meteorite.

If you stood in one place and tried to catch a meteorite, you'd probably still be waiting a billion years from now.

But a woman in Alabama was hit by one. She was napping on her living room couch one day when an 8½ pound (4 kilogram) meteorite came right through the roof of her house, bounced off the radio and struck her on the leg. She had only a minor bruise, and afterwards could boast that she was the only person in the United States—maybe in the whole world—ever to have been hit by a meteorite.

Even in space, where satellites and shuttles orbit Earth, there is not much danger of their being hit by meteoroids. So far they have been struck by nothing larger than small particles of dust. And already our spacecraft have traveled safely through the asteroid belt and beyond.

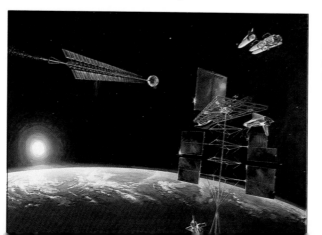

Spaceships on long space journeys will be outfitted with shields to protect them from meteorites.

How Hot Are Meteorites?

Suppose you saw a small meteorite fall from the sky and land on the ground. Would you run over and pick it up? Or would you think it might burn your hands?

Actually, it wouldn't be hot at all!

Some people in Sweden watched a meteorite land on a frozen lake. They were amazed that it didn't melt a hole in the ice.

Even very large meteorites, the kind that hit Earth in fiery crashes, aren't really very hot.

Remember that meteorites were once meteoroids. For millions of years they traveled in outer space, where the temperature is almost 500° below zero Fahrenheit (−260° Celsius). In its dash through Earth's atmosphere a meteor doesn't have time to heat up all the way through. The outer surfaces can burn, but the inside of a meteor stays cool. Once a meteor hits Earth and becomes a meteorite, its outer crust quickly cools off.

So if you reached out and touched a meteorite you had watched fall to Earth just minutes before, you might jerk your hand back all right. But not because the meteorite was too hot. You would probably be startled to find it so cold!

If you touched a newly-fallen meteorite, would you expect it to be hot?

A meteorite that landed on a frozen lake in Sweden didn't even melt a hole in the ice.

Meteorite Craters

When a giant meteor hits the ground, it makes a big hole. Very little of the meteorite will be found buried beneath this crater. Much of it turns to vapor. What is left is broken into fragments, some of them just particles of dust. These fragments, along with a lot of Earth soil and rock, are thrown out of the hole. That is why meteorite craters have a raised ring around them.

There are thousands of meteorite craters in the world. We are still discovering craters that were made millions of years ago.

Our knowledge of meteor craters is quite new. Not until late in the nineteenth century did scientists even know for sure that our planet had been hit by meteorites. Now we know that there are many meteor craters, some on every continent. Many have been discovered by airplanes and satellites taking pictures from high above the Earth. One of the largest, the Manicouagan Crater in Quebec, Canada, is a circular depression more than 40 miles (64 kilometers) across.

An aerial view of the largest meteorite crater in the United States, located near Winslow, Arizona.

The meteorite that made Meteor Crater, in the Arizona desert, may have weighed as much as a million tons!

The largest meteorite crater in the United States is in Arizona. It is almost 4,000 feet (more than 1,200 meters) across and about 570 feet (175 meters) deep. At first scientists thought that it had been made by a volcano. But rocks containing nickel and iron were found near the crater, and other scientists were sure they were pieces of a meteorite.

The crater also contained a lot of a glass-like material that is formed when sand is heated to at least 3,900° Fahrenheit (2,150° Celsius). Volcanos do not create heat that high. So it had to be an exploding meteorite that turned the sand into glass.

Scientists think the meteorite that made the Arizona crater hit the earth about 50,000 years ago. It may have weighed as much as 1 million tons (907,200 metric tons)!

If you ever climb up onto the rim of this Arizona crater and can look down into it, and then far across to the opposite side, try to imagine the tremendous explosion that made this gigantic hole in the desert.

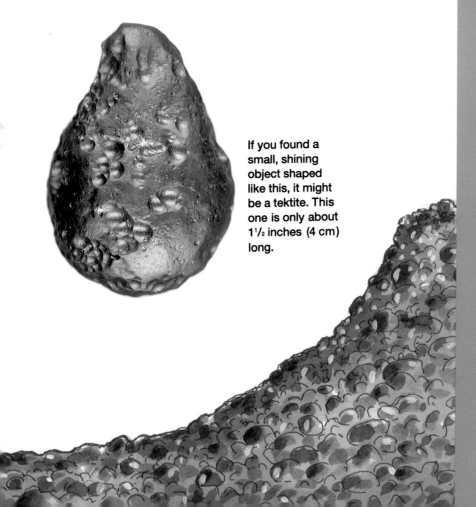

If you found a small, shining object shaped like this, it might be a tektite. This one is only about 1½ inches (4 cm) long.

SOLVING THE TEKTITE MYSTERY

If you visit a museum where there is an exhibit of meteorites, you might also see a display of small, shiny objects. Some might be shaped like buttons, others like spiralling cones or miniature dumbbells. They might be black, green, or amber in color. A label would tell you they are called tektites. What are tektites? Centuries ago, when these curious pieces were first picked up in Europe, people assumed they had been left there by ancient workers who had melted sand to make glass. But when these fragments were found on continents where glass had never been made, scientists began to take a new look at them. Where had these curiously shaped pieces of glass come from?

Volcanoes seemed like one possible source, but often tektites were found far from the sites of even the most ancient volcanic eruptions.

Were they little meteorites? For a while that seemed like a good explanation. But then it was discovered that they were made of Earth sand. Geologists quickly realized that, while the tektites were not meteorites themselves, there was a meteorite connection. If a large meteorite hits Earth in a sandy area, the heat melts the sand and sends molten globules of it flying through the air. The way these globules spin before they cool and drop back to Earth gives them their interesting shapes.

Meteor Showers

If you like to sleep out under the sky, and if you also like to watch for shooting stars, there is one week in the year that is better than any other time for doing both. That's the week of August 10 to 17. If you watch the sky on those nights, you are sure to see meteors—so many that we call their fall a meteor shower.

There are other times of the year when you can count on seeing meteor showers. But depending on where you live, it may be too cold at some of those times for you to want to spend a night outdoors waiting to see some shooting stars.

How do we know when there will be showers of meteors? We know because the orbits of meteor showers are the same as those of known comets. Since the paths of these comets have been carefully mapped, we know when the orbits of Earth and the comets cross each other.

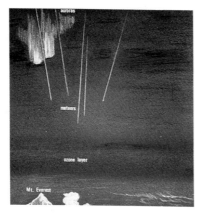

A meteor shower in the ozone layer.

In 1833 there was such an amazing meteor shower that the date on which it happened has since been called "the night the sky fell." People in the United States and sailors out on the Atlantic Ocean and in the Gulf of Mexico watched as more than 200,000 meteors streaked down from the sky. The date was November 13. If you watch the sky on that date and on the two nights before and after it, you will probably see a shower of meteors. But don't expect to see thousands. There might be just a few every hour. Never again have as many been seen as in November, 1833.

If you sleep out under the stars between August 10 and August 17 you will probably see many meteors streaking across the night sky.

18

The most famous meteor shower of all time occurred on November 13, 1833, a date known as "the night the sky fell."

TIMES WHEN YOU CAN SEE METEOR SHOWERS

When Earth passes through a swarm of meteors, the rocky chunks burn in our atmosphere and make a meteor shower, or become what we like to call "shooting stars." They do not come from a single point in space, although they seem to. In the list below, the dates of meteor showers are given first, then the names given to the particular showers, then the names of the constellations from which they appear to come.

January 1–6   Quadrantids Bootes
April 19–24   Lybrids   Lyra
May 1–8   Eta Aquarids Aquarius
July 25–August 18   Perseids Perseus
October 16–26   Orionids Orion
October 20–November 30 Taurids   Tauris
mid November   Leonids Leo
December 4–5   Phoenicids Phoenix
December 7–15   Geminids Gemini
December 17–24   Ursids Ursa Minor

Fireballs

Unlike meteor showers, which are silent and beautiful to watch, fireballs fill those who see them with fear. Fireball is the name we give to the very brightest meteors. They are so brilliant that when one appears, it may seem as bright as the sun.

Fireballs make frightening noises. People who have heard them describe the sound in different ways.

"It was like a train roaring toward me," say some people.

Others have said that a fireball sounded like many cannons being fired or the loudest claps of thunder they had ever heard. Or, worse, like many hissing snakes.

Most fireballs burn up or explode in the atmosphere. Few drop any pieces onto the ground. The dust-like particles that remain after the explosion are soon scattered by the wind. When meteorites are found after a fireball is seen, the people who find them are usually surprised at their small size. While the fireball in the sky may have looked as big as a football stadium, the meteorite may be more the size of a football.

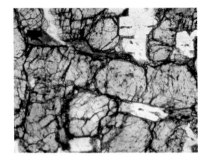

These two photographs are of the same meteorite slice, taken through a microscope under different lighting conditions. The meteorite, known as Zagami, was found in Nigeria and is believed to be a piece of Mars.

In 1976, there was a spectacular fireball display in the sky over China.

Huge fireballs often break up into pieces no larger than coins.

A fireball can make a roar greater than the loudest thunder you have ever heard.

FAMOUS TWENTIETH CENTURY FIREBALLS

The Mysterious Fireball Parade

In March, 1913, thousands of people saw two sets of fireballs streak across the sky above Canada, the United States, the Atlantic Ocean, and then Brazil. Many objects appeared to be moving in formation. No meteorite fragments were ever found after this strange sighting.

The Stone That Fell on Paragould

On a cold February night in 1930, residents of Illinois, Missouri, and Arkansas were awakened by bright lights and loud noises. Later, an 820-pound (370 kilogram) stony meteorite was found in a field near Paragould, Arkansas. At the time, it was the largest stone meteorite ever recovered after having been seen flashing by overhead.

Explosion Over Siberia

In 1947, a huge explosion and fireball broke windows in an area more than 100 miles (160 kilometers) wide in Siberia. Trees were knocked down and stripped of their leaves. Scientists later found a hill which had been hit by numerous meteorites.

Meteorite Fireworks Above China

In 1976, many thousands of people watched a heavenly display in the sky above northeastern China. The meteorite that caused it broke into many separate, fiery pieces. One of them, weighing almost two tons (1.8 metric tons), was later dug up from a depth of 18 feet (5.5 meters).

21

Why Did the Dinosaurs Die?

Did a meteorite kill off the dinosaurs? Many scientists today think the answer is yes. They believe that this is the way it happened:

About 65 million years ago a huge meteorite, or maybe several of them, slammed into Earth and exploded. All over the world forests and grasses burned and animals died.

For many months, long after the fires had gone out, the air was filled with soot and ash. They kept the sun's light and warmth from reaching our planet. Earth was cold and dark. Because of their big size, dinosaurs needed a lot of food. But the plants they once ate no longer grew. Any dinosaurs that had not been killed by the blast or the fires soon starved to death. The age of the dinosaurs came to an end.

Have you ever seen a cliff and noticed stripes in it? They are made by layers of dirt and rock that formed at different times in Earth's past. When scientists studied cliffs in various parts of the world, they found something surprising. About 65 million years ago, at the same time the dinosaurs died, a layer of soot and ash was deposited on the surface of the earth. That had to mean there were great fires at that time.

In this same layer the scientists discovered iridium. Iridium is a very rare metal. On Earth it is buried deep in the ground. But it is also found in meteorites. The scientists feel sure that the iridium, soot, and ash were the result of huge meteorites hitting Earth's surface. And they believe that that is what led to the death of the dinosaurs.

Scientists have searched for years for a crater that might account for such a catastrophe. Many now think they have found it, on the edge of the Yucatan Peninsula in Mexico. Even though it is now buried under rock and the waters of the Caribbean Sea, studies have told them it is almost 112 miles (180 kilometers) across!

Maybe you have a meteorite to thank for your being here at all. For human beings probably could not have survived in a world filled with huge prehistoric beasts.

We learn a lot about dinosaurs by studying their bones.

A gigantic meteorite striking Earth may have brought an end to the Age of Dinosaurs.

The Arctic Giant

The Greenland Eskimos made spear points out of pieces they chipped off meteorites.

In 1897, the American explorer, Robert Peary, went to Greenland to get a meteorite. Three years earlier the Eskimos had shown him the big black rock. It had fallen from the sky long ago, they said, along with two other smaller rocks.

The Eskimos called the two smaller ones "The Woman" and "The Dog." The largest one they called "The Tent." In their language the name for it was "Ahnighito."

Peary had been able to take the two smaller meteorites to New York on a second visit. Now he had come back for Ahnighito. It was only about 300 feet (90 meters) inland from a bay where he could anchor his ship. Still, Peary knew that moving the great rock to his ship and getting it aboard would not be easy.

Peary had come well prepared. He had brought along giant logs and square timbers. The strongest of the Eskimos and Peary's men were able to tip Ahnighito up just enough to get the first of the logs and timbers under it. Gradually, they built a sort of movable roadway. The timbers pointed toward the shore, the round logs lay across them. Men and dogs pulled on heavy chains to move Ahnighito forward on the round log rollers. When Ahnighito rested on the first rollers, the ones at the back, no longer bearing its weight, were moved up front. Finally, Ahnighito was at the water's edge.

It was only August, but already the first winter snows had begun. Now a fierce storm raged. Lashed by snow, wind and waves, Peary and his men built a ramp between the rock and the ship. The Eskimos watched from shore. They were afraid that the huge waves, the crashing icebergs, and the weight of Ahnighito would sink the ship.

When the chains that bound the meteorite were attached to the ship's steam-powered winch, the mighty rock moved slowly up the ramp and onto the ship.

Peary knew he had no time to waste. Winter could lock his ship in the ice for months. He had to get out of the bay fast. He rammed his ship between the towering blocks of ice and out onto the open sea.

His troubles still weren't over. His compass wasn't working. The iron in the meteorite attracted the needle so that it no longer pointed to the north. To keep from getting lost, Peary had to stay close to shore. Following the curving coast used more of the ship's fuel than he had figured. He barely made it to a port in Labrador, where he took on more coal.

It was a difficult journey, but the good ship *Hope* safely carried the large meteorite Ahnighito from Greenland to New York.

There was great excitement in New York when Peary's ship finally docked. A crane lifted the meteorite off onto a scale that had been specially built to hold the great rock. It weighed 68,000 pounds (31,000 kilograms), as much as six full-grown elephants! Everybody cheered. Children were allowed to climb up onto Ahnighito and have their pictures taken.

It took eighty horses to haul the meteorite through the city streets to the American Museum of Natural History.

After Ahnighito was unloaded from the ship, boys climbed up onto it to have their pictures taken.

Millions of people have come to see and touch this wondrous stone from space and to hear the story of how it was brought to New York.

Peary was famous for the journey he made with the giant meteorite. He became even more famous for a journey he made later. For the Robert Peary who brought Ahnighito from Greenland to the United States is the same Robert Peary, by then an Admiral in the U.S. Navy, who was the the first man to reach the North Pole.

LOST METEORITES

The Lost Meteorite of Gran Chaco
One of the world's largest iron meteorites was found and then lost in the rugged hill country of Argentina. It was discovered in 1783 by Spaniards looking for a silver mine. They dug around the huge rock to try to find out just how big it was. They said afterwards that it probably weighed 50,000 pounds (22,700 kilograms). The trouble was that, while they were digging, they accidentally rolled the meteorite into a nearby hollow. Many expeditions have returned to the area to search for the Gran Chaco stone, but it has never been found again.

The Oregon Phantom
A large stony meteorite was discovered in 1858 by Dr. John Evans, a geologist and surveyor. He described its location as being high up on a treeless slope of Bald Mountain in Oregon. Dr. Evans died before he could lead an expedition to recover the meteorite. Today nobody is sure where "Bald Mountain" is, and, although thousands of scientists and amateurs have searched for the Oregon Phantom, it has never been seen again.

The Great Chinguetti Iron
If it really exists, this African meteorite is the world's largest. It is believed that Bedouin tribesmen of the western Sahara Desert know its location. The only outsider to see it was led to it, in 1916, with a blindfold over his eyes. He reported that it was 300 feet (91 meters) long and more than 100 feet (30 meters) high. If that description is correct, scientists figure that the Great Chinguetti Iron must weigh more than 1 million tons (907,000 metric tons)!

27

The Siberian Mystery

What is the largest meteorite ever to land on Earth? Since meteorites have been striking our planet for many millions of years, long before there were any people, no one can answer that question.

The greatest meteorite that we know about for sure is called the Tunguska meteorite. It exploded above Siberia on the last day of June in 1908.

People almost 500 miles (800 kilometers) away saw a fireball streak across the sky.

"It was brighter than the sun," said frightened Siberian peasants. One man, fifty miles from the blast, said the heat was so great that he tore at his shirt, thinking it was on fire.

More than 3,000 miles (4,800 kilometers) away, seismographs, devices that detect earthquakes, registered the impact.

For a long time afterward, people all over Europe and Asia saw strange and beautiful sunsets, with bands of bright red and yellow and green. Scientists knew that the brilliant colors were caused by dust in the atmosphere, but even they did not know where the dust had come from.

The heat created by the Siberian meteorite was so great that people many miles away thought their clothes were on fire.

Russian scientists investigating the Siberian crash site were shocked to see that miles and miles of once-green forest had been totally destroyed.

It wasn't until almost twenty years later that a group of Russian scientists was sent to Siberia to see what they could learn about the mysterious explosion. After a long and difficult journey through unmapped forest, they came upon a shocking sight. As far as they could see, the forest had been leveled. Huge trees had been knocked down as though they were matchsticks. Everything was burned. The blackened ground was pitted with craters.

Since then many expeditions have gone to study the area. One of the clues found near some of the craters were tiny diamond-like stones. Such stones are formed only under tremendous pressure. They had been discovered before in places where meteorites had collided with Earth.

Yet many people felt that something other than a meteorite had exploded in that wild and lonely place. Some thought it was a comet. Others even wondered if it might have been an alien space ship.

To this day there is disagreement about what happened in the Siberian wilderness. But, in 1980, 72 years after the Tunguska explosion, a group of scientists announced they were sure that it was a meteorite that had destroyed that great stretch of forest.

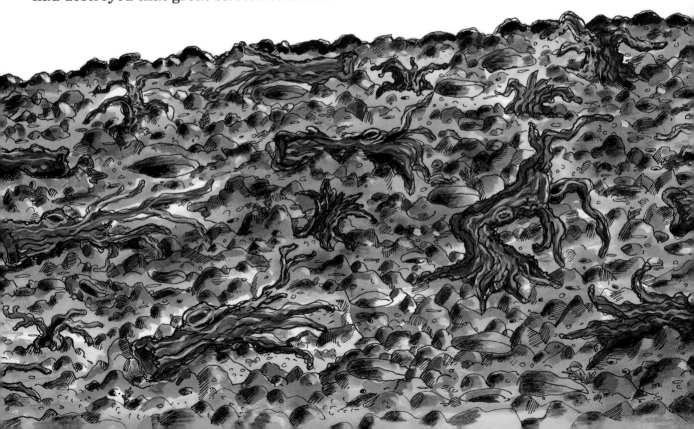

If You Find a Meteorite

Would you like to search for meteorites? In the United States more meteorites have been found in Kansas than in any other state, but they can be found almost anywhere.

How would you know a meteorite if you saw one? Many look so much like Earth rocks that it's hard to recognize them. It's a lot easier to find meteorites in the fields of the midwest than it is to spot them in more rocky parts of the country, such as New England. Yet meteorites are found in the New England states, some of them piled in the walls early farmers made with the stones they dug out of their fields.

If you can visit a museum that has a display of meteorites look carefully at the different kinds. You will see that the iron meteorites are dark, with a definite metallic look. They may even be rusty. They are usually rough and have irregular shapes. The surface of an iron meteorite is pitted, as if at some time the rock had been soft and someone had pushed thumbs or fingers into it.

Stony-irons are usually about half iron, half stone. Their surfaces are also pitted. Newly fallen ones are blackish; older falls are yellowish to brown.

Stony meteorites are a rusty brown if they are old, but have a burnt, blackish, pebbly crust if their fall was recent. Stony meteorites look the most like Earth rocks.

Meteorite hunters often use a metal detector to help in the search.

Perhaps this young person is thinking about the long journey this meteorite made through the dark and cold of space.

If you ever find what you think might be a meteorite, you could take it to someone who teaches science at a school or college near where you live. If the teacher or professor does not know what you have found, he or she could tell you how to find out. There are laboratories to which you can send a piece of rock to be analyzed.

Many people collect meteorites for a hobby, so you might want to keep any meteorites you find. Or you could give them to your school or to a museum.

Maybe a meteorite you find will help scientists discover some of the secrets locked in stardust.

This scientist is using a powerful electron microscope to probe the mysteries of meteorites. He may find answers to some of the questions about how our universe was formed.

Index